THE KIDS BIBLE

LEENA LANE

— AND —

GILLIAN CHAPMAN

CONCORDIA PUBLISHING HOUSE · SAINT LOUIS

Contents

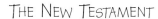

THE NEW TESTAMENT

In the beginning

Genesis 1–2

At the beginning of time, God made the light and the darkness.

God made big, tall mountains and deep, blue seas.

God made plants and flowers and trees and filled the land with them.

God made the round, spinning earth, the red-hot sun, and the silvery moon. He made twinkling stars and planets.

God filled the sea with slippery, shiny fish and the air with birds that chatter and sing.

God filled the land with animals of every kind— tall and short, prickly and furry, striped and spotted and patterned.

"Now I will make people," said God. God made Adam and Eve — a man and a woman who could think and feel and love. He made them in His image, which means they were like Him. He made a beautiful garden for them to live in called the Garden of Eden.

God was pleased with everything He had made. It was very good.

Noah's ark

Genesis 3; 6:5–8:22

God had made a beautiful world, but it wasn't long before the people He made sinned. Adam and Eve did not do as God told them. They ate the fruit of a tree that God told them to leave alone. So they had to leave the Garden of Eden. After the time of Adam and Eve, the earth became filled with many, many people. Some obeyed God. But more did not.

God was sad about how wicked the world had become. God was sad about sin.

God was going to send a great flood. But God remembered Noah. Noah loved God. Noah also sinned, but he believed in God's forgiveness.

God planned to save Noah, his wife, his three sons, and their wives. He told Noah to build a huge boat called an ark and to fill it with two of every kind of animal on the earth. Noah covered it with tar to keep out the water.

It would float on the waters until the flood was over. Noah trusted God. He packed food for his family and all the animals. Then it began to rain. It rained and rained for forty days and nights. The waters covered the earth. But the ark floated. God kept Noah safe.

At last the rain stopped and dry land appeared. The ark came to rest on the mountains of Ararat. When the land was dry enough, Noah and his family and all the animals came out of the ark. God had saved them.

God put a rainbow in the sky as a promise that there would never be a flood to cover the whole earth again.

God's promise to Abraham

Genesis 12:1–3; 15:1–6; 21:1–6

Abram and his wife, Sarai, lived in the city of Haran. Abram loved God. God said Abram was His friend. God told Abram to leave his home. So he left his home to settle in a new land that God had showed him. "I will make your family into a great nation and I will bless you," God told him.

The problem was Abram and his wife, Sarai, could not have children. Without children, their family could not grow any bigger.

But one day God told Abram that he would have a son and a very large family.

"Look at the stars and try to count them," said God. "You will have as many people in your family as the number of stars you see."

Abram trusted God and believed His special promise.

Then, when Abram was 99 years old, God's promise came true!

God gave Abram and his wife new names — Abraham and Sarah. Sarah gave birth to a son. They were so happy, they named him "Isaac," which means "laughter." God had kept His promise to Abraham and Sarah.

God keeps His promises to us too. He helps us celebrate another promise He made and kept. He sent Jesus to be our Savior.

Rebekah's kindness

Genesis 24

When Isaac grew up, Abraham sent a servant to his homeland to find a wife for Isaac. The servant took with him ten camels.

After a long hot journey, he stopped by a well to drink. He prayed to God for help: "I will ask a girl to give me a drink. Let her be the one you want Isaac to marry."

Before the servant had finished praying, Rebekah came to fetch water from the well for her family. She was very beautiful.

She noticed the servant standing at the well with his camels.

"Please give me a drink," he said.

Rebekah offered him some water and then gave the ten camels a drink too. They were very thirsty.

Then the servant gave her gold bracelets and other presents.

"Who is your father?" asked the servant. "Is there room at your house for me and the camels to stay tonight?"

"His name is Bethuel," said Rebekah. The servant knew that Bethuel was a relative of Abraham. So they went to see Rebekah's family.

That evening, the servant told Rebekah's father that he had come to find a wife for Abraham's son, Isaac. He asked if Rebekah would be Isaac's wife. She agreed and set off the next day to marry Isaac. God showed His love and care for Isaac by giving him a wife. God shows His love and care for us too.

11

Jacob and Esau

Genesis 25:19–34; 27; 33:1–4

Isaac and Rebekah had twin sons called Esau and Jacob. They were very different!

Esau had red hair and was very hairy. He was a skillful hunter and loved being outdoors with his bow and arrows.

Jacob was a quiet man who liked staying at home with his mother, Rebekah. He loved cooking. He had a big cooking pot and made wonderful soups and stews in it for all the family.

Esau was born first, which would usually mean that when his father died, Esau would be given all that his father owned and a special blessing. But when the boys were born, God told Rebekah that the younger son, Jacob, would receive a special blessing called a birthright.

One day, when Esau came home from hunting, he was very hungry. He could smell a delicious stew that Jacob had been cooking.

"Give me some of that stew," Esau said to Jacob.

"Only if you promise to let me be the one who gets the birthright blessing" said Jacob. The birthright blessing would give Jacob all the promises that God had made to his father, Isaac, and to his grandfather, Abraham.

Esau couldn't resist the stew any longer, so he promised to let Jacob have their father's blessing and all he owned. Esau cared only about his hungry tummy!

Jacob used a trick because he couldn't wait for God to work out His plan.

When their father, Isaac, was very old and almost blind, Jacob pretended to be Esau and tricked his father into giving him a blessing.

Esau was so angry, Jacob had to run away from home!

God was not happy with Jacob or Esau. They both needed God's forgiveness. They had done wrong things. But God is faithful. He kept His promise to love and bless Jacob. God helped Esau to forgive his brother. Many years later the two brothers met again. God helped them to be friends again.

13

Jacob's favorite son

Genesis 37

Jacob had a large family of 12 sons and a daughter. Jacob loved all his children, but his favorite was Joseph. When Joseph was 17 years old, his father gave him a very special present. He gave him a wonderful coat to wear.

Joseph was very pleased with his coat and walked around proudly in front of his brothers. "Look at me!" he said. "Dad's given me this coat!"

But his brothers were jealous. Why did their father love Joseph more than he loved them? Why couldn't they all have a splendid coat?

They didn't want Joseph to be more important than they were.

To make matters even worse, Joseph started telling them about some strange dreams he had been having.

He dreamed that there were 11 sheaves of grain all bowing down to his sheaf. And then he dreamed he saw 11 stars, the sun, and the moon, all bowing to his star. His brothers were furious.

One day when the brothers were in the fields looking after their father's sheep and goats, they decided what to do. The brothers threw Joseph into an empty well! They were going to leave him there, but then they saw a group of traveling traders on their way to Egypt. The brothers decided to sell Joseph to the traders. So Joseph was taken to Egypt to be a slave.

The brothers thought they would never see Joseph again. But God had plans for Joseph. He would help his brothers and many others. God has plans for us too, even when we have troubles.

Joseph in Egypt

Genesis 39–47

When Joseph arrived in Egypt, he was bought by the captain of the guard, Potiphar. Joseph worked hard for his new master. Potiphar was pleased with Joseph and soon put him in charge of his household.

But Potiphar's wife told lies about Joseph, and he was thrown into prison.

In prison Joseph met the king's chief baker and the king's wine steward. They were prisoners too.

One night, they had unusual dreams. God helped Joseph understand what the dreams meant. The wine steward spoke first. "I dreamt that there was a grapevine with three branches. The grapes ripened and I squeezed them into the king's cup and gave it to him to drink."

Joseph said, "In three days the king will let you out of prison and give you back your old job. Please remember me when you are out of prison and tell the king about me."

Next it was the baker's turn. "I was carrying three breadbaskets on my head. In the top basket were all sorts of pastries for the king, and the birds were eating them all up."

Joseph told him: "In three days the king will let you out of prison, but he will cut off your head."

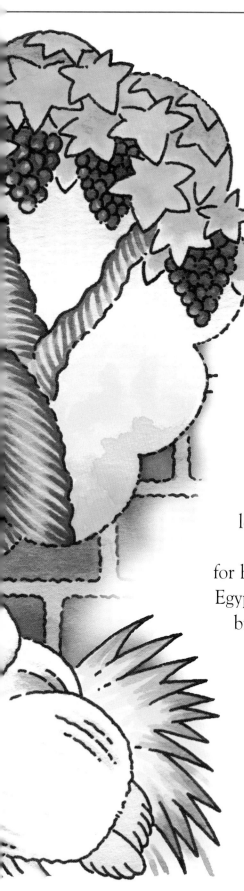

The poor baker was very worried.

But it all happened just as Joseph had said.

Two years later, the king began to have strange dreams that no one understood. The king's wine steward told the king about Joseph. God helped Joseph tell the king what his dreams meant. The king made Joseph into an important leader in Egypt.

One day, Joseph's brothers came to Egypt to beg for help. There was no more food in their land and Egypt had plenty. They did not recognize their lost brother as the great man before them. When Joseph told them who he was, they were afraid Joseph would want to punish them. Instead Joseph was happy. He began to cry and gave each of them a hug.

God helped Joseph to forgive his brothers. Then his whole family came to live in Egypt. They were all together again at last.

God looked after Joseph through all his troubles. And He looks after us too.

The baby in the basket

Exodus 2:1–10

While Joseph was alive, his family lived happily in Egypt. But after his death, new kings came who didn't know how God had blessed him. Joseph's children became slaves in Egypt. And the new king was a very cruel man.

Soon there were so many slaves that the king began to fear them. So he ordered all the baby boys to be thrown into the river and drowned.

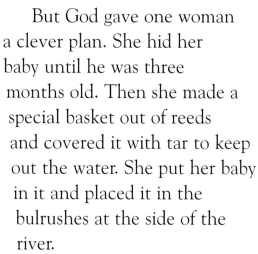

But God gave one woman a clever plan. She hid her baby until he was three months old. Then she made a special basket out of reeds and covered it with tar to keep out the water. She put her baby in it and placed it in the bulrushes at the side of the river.

The baby's sister, Miriam, watched close by.

A little while later, the king's daughter came to the river. She saw the basket, heard a tiny noise, and found the baby inside. The princess wanted to help him.

Miriam stepped out from the bulrushes.

"I know who can nurse the baby," said Miriam. And she fetched her own mother.

The baby was called Moses. God provided care for Moses. He was looked after by his mother until he was old enough to live in the palace with the princess. God also cares for us at all times.

The plagues of Egypt

Exodus 3–12

When Moses grew up, he was upset to see how badly the cruel king treated his slaves. Moses ran away from the palace and became a shepherd in Midian.

One day, as Moses was looking after some sheep, he saw a strange sight. A bush appeared to be on fire, yet it did not burn up. Moses went to have a closer look. Suddenly, God spoke from the bush! "Moses," said God, "I have heard My people crying out to Me for help. I have come to rescue them from the cruel Egyptians and take them to a new land of their own, flowing with milk and honey. I am sending you to bring My people out of Egypt."

Moses was afraid but God promised to help him. Moses went to the king of Egypt and told him to let God's people go. But the king would not listen.

So Moses warned him that there would be terrible plagues. The river turned to blood; the land was covered in frogs; locusts ate all the crops; many Egyptian animals died of disease; the people were covered in painful sores; hailstorms

battered the land; and Egypt was plunged into darkness.

Still the king would not change his mind.

Finally God sent the most terrible plague of all. The firstborn sons of Egypt would die, including the king's son. But God kept the Israelites safe. He told them to paint their doorways with blood from a lamb then eat a special meal of lamb, bitter herbs, and bread without yeast.

"You must remember this night forever," said God. It was called Passover, when death passed over the houses of the Israelites and God kept them safe.

That night, the firstborn sons of Egypt were killed. The king's own son died.

"Go and leave Egypt!" the king said in despair.

So Moses led his people out of Egypt on a long journey toward the new land that God had promised to them.

God worked to save His people in Egypt. God worked through our Savior, Jesus. Through His saving grace, Jesus makes us God's people.

Moses crosses the Red Sea

Exodus 13:17–14:31; 16–20; Deuteronomy 34:1–2

Moses led God's people out of Egypt, but the king changed his mind! He ordered the Egyptian army to follow them with chariots and horses.

Moses and the people camped by the Red Sea. When they saw the army coming, they were terrified. But Moses said, "Don't be afraid! God will help us."

God told Moses to walk toward the Red Sea with his stick held high.

Then God sent a strong wind that blew the water back. Dry ground appeared between two walls of water. Moses led his people across a dry path to safety on the other side of the Red Sea.

The Egyptian army tried to follow, but their chariot wheels got stuck in the ground. God told Moses to hold out his hand over the water. The sea came crashing down over the Egyptian army. All the soldiers were drowned.

Moses led the people on toward the promised land.

But there were troubles ahead. They wandered in the wilderness for forty years.

God spoke to Moses many times. God wanted His people to trust Him. He lovingly provided special food and drink for them every day. He gave Moses the Ten Commandments on stone tablets, telling the people how to live.

Moses never entered the promised land, but God showed him the land from a mountaintop before he died. God had been faithful to Moses no matter where he went. And God does the same thing for us, especially as He guides us to heaven through Jesus.

Joshua and the walls of Jericho

Joshua 1; 6

After Moses died, God chose Joshua to lead God's people to the promised land. But first they had to get past the city of Jericho.

The city had huge, thick, stone walls. It seemed impossible to get through. But God had a plan. God told Joshua to choose seven priests with trumpets made of rams' horns. God said to march around the city once every day for six days, blowing their trumpets and following the golden ark of the covenant, which held the stone tablets God had given to Moses.

On the seventh day, the priests had to march around the city six times. Then, on the seventh time, the priests sounded a long trumpet blast on their horns, the people shouted, and... the mighty walls of Jericho fell to the ground.

God had given them the city.

Praise God! He helped His people during bad times.

Praise God! Through Jesus, He helps us overcome evil.

Gideon's victory

Judges 6–7

When Joshua died, the Israelite people began to turn away from God and His commandments. This made God angry. Armies from other countries came to fight against the Israelites. Finally, God sent judges to guide and help the Israelites. One of the judges was Gideon.

God had chosen Gideon to lead the army. God had a special plan to defeat the Midianite army. God's plan used no weapons.

Instead, Gideon gave each soldier a trumpet and a jar with a burning torch inside.

"This is what we must do," he told his army. "When I get to the edge of the camp, watch me and copy what I do. When I blow my trumpet, blow yours too and shout, 'A sword for the LORD and for Gideon!'"

So Gideon and his men came to the edge of the camp in the middle of the night. After Gideon's signal, everyone broke their jars, picked up their trumpets, and shouted: "A sword for the LORD and for Gideon!"

The enemy army was surprised and confused. God's plan worked. He had helped Gideon win the battle. Gideon and his people gave thanks to God, who made the victory possible.

Just as God had an important plan for Gideon, we can be sure He has plans for us.

The strength of Samson

Judges 13–16

Even after all God had done for them, the Israelites again turned away from God. So for forty years they were attacked by the fearsome Philistine army.

God sent another judge to the people to try to save the Israelites from the Philistines. He was called Samson.

Samson was a very, very strong man. He once fought a lion and killed it with his own hands! God had made him strong. Nobody knew the secret of his great strength.

One day Samson met a woman called Delilah. The Philistines paid her to find out the secret of his strength. Delilah kept asking Samson until finally he could stand it no longer.

"If I cut off my hair, I will be made weak," said Samson.

So when Samson was asleep, Delilah called to his enemies and they cut off his hair. At once his strength left him. He was blinded and thrown into prison in chains.

But Samson's hair began to grow again…

The Philistines had a feast in the temple to their god Dagon. They brought Samson from prison to entertain them. In humility, Samson prayed to God

to remember him and to give him back his strength one more time. God heard Samson's prayer. He helped Samson push over the pillars of the temple.

The roof fell and all the Philistines were killed. Samson died too, but God helped him save the Israelites from the power of the Philistine enemies.

25

David plays for King Saul

1 Samuel 8–10; 16

The Israelites wanted God to give them a king. "We want to have a king like all the other nations," they said, "someone to lead us in battle." They asked a wise prophet called Samuel to find a king for them.

The first king of Israel was called Saul. Samuel anointed him as king by pouring oil over his head. "Long live the king!" shouted the people.

At first Saul listened to God and tried to be a good king. He led his armies into battle against their enemies. But later Saul did not do as God told him, and God became angry.

God told Samuel to go to Bethlehem and find the sons of Jesse. The youngest one, David, was anointed to be king after Saul's death.

26

King Saul became a very troubled man since he had not done what God had told him to do. Now he often sat in his room feeling terrible. His servants thought that it might help him to listen to some music.

"There is a boy in Bethlehem," said one servant, "who is very good at playing the harp. His name is David. He takes care of his father's sheep."

Saul asked them to fetch David. Saul did not know that David had been anointed to be the next king.

David set off from home with a young goat, a donkey, food, and drink.

He arrived at the king's tent and went to see the king, ready to play his harp.

King Saul listened to him playing the harp and suddenly felt much better. God used David's music to calm King Saul's troubled spirit.

"Stay here," he said to David. "I wish to hear more."

So David was brought into the king's service. Whenever the king felt terrible, David would play beautiful music on his harp.

David and Goliath

1 Samuel 17–19; 2 Samuel 3:1–5; 1 Kings 1:28–6:38

Who could fight a giant?

Goliath, the champion of the Philistine army, asked King Saul to find a man who would fight him. But Goliath was more than nine feet tall! No one in Saul's army even dared to try!

For forty days, Goliath asked the army, "Who will fight me?"

Then one day, David left his sheep to take some food to his brothers, who were soldiers in the camp.

David heard Goliath shouting. He couldn't understand why no one stepped forward. David had often fought wild animals to protect his sheep.

"God will help me fight Goliath," said David, "just as He has helped me protect my sheep."

"Then put on my armor and take my sword," King Saul said. But they were much too heavy for David.

28

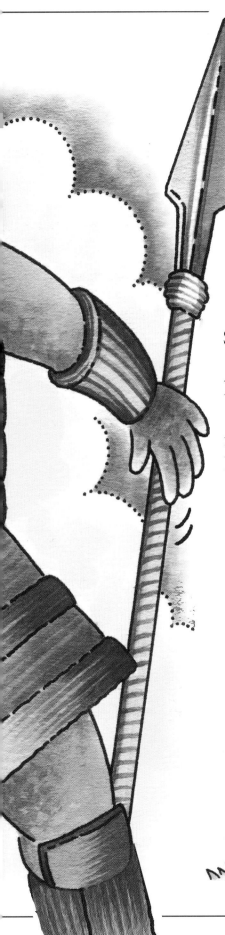

God gave David a different plan. David went to the river and chose five smooth stones. He took out his sling, then set off to face Goliath. David called on God's help as he faced Goliath. With a quick flick of his wrist, he whirled the sling around his head and threw one of the stones at Goliath. It hit him on the forehead and killed the giant!

The Philistines turned and ran away, chased by King Saul's army. God had given the Israelites a victory!

Everyone loved David and called him a hero. This made King Saul very jealous. For the rest of his life, Saul tried to kill David.

But after Saul's death, David became God's chosen king of Israel.

During King David's reign, God grew Israel into a mighty nation. David's son, Solomon, became the next king. God made him very wise and helped Solomon build a magnificent temple for God.

Elijah

1 Kings 16:29–18:48

After Solomon, many kings did not follow God's ways. One bad king was called Ahab.

King Ahab built a temple and altars for another god called Baal. This made God very angry.

Elijah was a prophet. God gave him messages for the people. God told Elijah to go see the king.

"Ahab!" said Elijah. "There is going to be a terrible drought for many years. The rain will come only when I say."

Ahab and his wife were trying to kill all God's prophets. Elijah was now in danger. So God told Elijah to run to the east and hide in the Kerith Ravine.

God ordered ravens to bring Elijah bread and meat every morning and evening. Elijah drank the cool water from the brook in the ravine until it dried up.

Then God told Elijah to go to Zarephath, where a widow offered him all she had—a handful of flour in a jar and a little oil.

Elijah told the widow to make a small loaf of bread. "God says the jar of flour and the jug of oil will never be empty until the day the rains come again!" said Elijah. This is exactly what happened.

After more than three years of drought, God told Elijah to return to see King Ahab.

Elijah spoke boldly: "You have turned away from God and worshiped Baal instead. Let's have a contest to see who is the true God. Bring all the prophets of Baal to Mount Carmel," said Elijah.

30

"Get two bulls. The prophets of Baal will put one bull on their altar. I will put the other bull on the altar of the Lord. Then the prophets of Baal can call upon their gods, and I will call upon my God to send fire to burn up the bulls. Whoever answers with fire is the true God."

The prophets of Baal shouted all day long, but there was no fire.

"Shout louder!" said Elijah, "Perhaps Baal is asleep!"

But no fire came.

Then Elijah put the bull on the altar of the Lord. "Now fill four large jars with water and pour it on top," he said to the servants, "Do it three times!" Soon the altar was soaked with water.

Elijah stepped forward and prayed: "Oh, Lord God, please answer me. Show these people that You are the real God. Turn them back to You again."

Suddenly God sent fire to burn up the bull on the altar and all the water around it. Everyone bowed down, shouting, "The Lord is God!"

"Go and eat and drink, Ahab!" said Elijah to the king, "There is the sound of heavy rain."

A small raincloud appeared in the sky. Soon the rains fell again. God had sent fire and rain and shown that He was the true God.

God heard Elijah's prayers and helped him.

God hears and answers our prayers too.

Thrown to the lions!

Daniel 1; 6

Many years later, King Nebuchadnezzar of Babylon came to Jerusalem and held it captive. He took away treasures from the Temple of God. Nebuchadnezzar also commanded that some of Israel's handsome young men should serve in the royal household in Babylon. One of these men was called Daniel. He was taken far away from his home.

Daniel loved God and prayed to Him, but the people around him didn't like it.

Daniel worked hard and the king made him a leader. But Daniel's enemies were jealous and plotted against him. The mean men asked the king to make a rule that no one should pray to anyone but the king for thirty days or they would be thrown into a pit of lions. Daniel trusted God to help him and still prayed to God.

Daniel was arrested and taken to be fed to the lions!

The king was horrified, but he hoped that Daniel's God would rescue him.

As soon as morning came, the king went back to the lions' pit and called, "Daniel! Has your God saved you?"

Daniel called back, "Yes! I'm alive!" God had sent an angel to stop the lions from harming him.

The king released Daniel and punished the men who had tried to hurt him. The king commanded all his people to honor Daniel's God: "He is the living God, who has rescued Daniel from the lions!"

So Daniel was free to pray to God for the rest of his life.

Just as God helped Daniel, He wants to help us every day in everything we do.

Jonah and the big fish

Jonah 1–3

The people of Nineveh were very sinful. God told Jonah to go to Nineveh and tell the people that He was angry with them. But Jonah was afraid, and he didn't want to do it! So he went on a ship and set sail for a distant shore in the opposite direction. He was running away from God. But Jonah couldn't hide.

God sent a mighty storm so bad that the sailors thought they would all drown.

"It's my fault!" said Jonah. "I ran away from God! You must throw me into the sea!"

At first the sailors didn't want to throw Jonah overboard. But the storm became worse until they were in great danger. So they threw Jonah out of the boat.

The storm stopped as soon as Jonah sank down into the dark water.

But God saved Jonah from drowning.

He sent an enormous fish to come and swallow up Jonah.

Inside the fish, Jonah prayed to God. "Thank You for saving me!" he prayed. "You are a great God."

Jonah stayed inside the fish for three days and three nights. It was very dark and smelly. Then the fish spat him out onto a beach.

"Now go to Nineveh!" said God. This time Jonah did as God had asked him and the people repented.

By sending Jonah, God wanted to show His love for all the people of Nineveh. God gave them a chance to say they were sorry for their sins, and He forgave them.

God wants all people to be saved, and He helps us to tell the message of His love to others.

Jesus is born

Matthew 1:18–24; Luke 1:26–2:1–7

God had promised to send a Savior to His people. No one knew when He would come, but many people were waiting.

God sent the angel Gabriel to a town called Nazareth. He had come to tell Mary that God had chosen her for a very special purpose. She would have a baby named Jesus.

"Jesus will be very important. He will be the Son of God!" said the angel. Mary sang praises to God for choosing her to be the mother of God's Son!

Mary was soon to be married to Joseph. Joseph's family came from Bethlehem.

Shortly before Mary's baby was due to be born, Joseph had to return to Bethlehem to be counted by the Roman governor. Mary had to go too.

It was a very long, tiring journey. Joseph walked in front with Mary a little way behind. Their donkey carried their small bundles of clothes and a water bottle.

When they arrived in Bethlehem, the town was full of other visitors. There was nowhere to stay! Joseph knocked on many doors in the town, trying to find a room for them to sleep. At last an inn-keeper said they could stay in a stable where the animals slept. There was no bed, but it was warm and dry in the straw.

Jesus was born. Mary laid the new baby, the Son of God, in a manger on the soft hay.

God had kept His promise to send the world a Savior.

The shepherds' surprise

Luke 2:8–20

On the hills near Bethlehem, a group of shepherds was looking after their sheep.

It was night, and they had to make sure that no wild animals came to snatch their sheep away.

The shepherds camped around a fire to keep them warm. They began to feel a bit sleepy.

Suddenly there was a blinding flash in the sky. An angel appeared!

"Don't be afraid!" the angel said. "I come to bring you good news. This very night a baby has been born in Bethlehem. He is Christ the Lord! You will find the baby wrapped in strips of cloth and lying in a manger. Go now and see Him!"

The shepherds could not speak—they were both very frightened and amazed.

Then many angels appeared in the sky, singing, "Glory to God in the highest, and on earth peace to men!" It was a beautiful sound.

"Hurry, hurry!" shouted the shepherds. "We must go to Bethlehem at once to find the baby God has told us about!"

They hurried through the town, looking for a newborn baby. They found Mary and Joseph. There, in a manger, wrapped up in cloths, was the newborn baby: Jesus, the Savior of all. The shepherds looked at the tiny baby and they felt great joy in their hearts.

When they had said good-bye, they hurried into the town, telling everyone they met: "We've seen the Savior!" They danced and sang songs to God for keeping His promise to send a Savior. They were praising God for all they had seen. It had been just as the angel had said.

That Savior, Jesus, was born for me and for you and for everyone. God's love is great!

Following the star

Matthew 2:1–12

When Jesus was born in Bethlehem, Wise Men in lands far away saw a very bright star in the sky. They knew it meant that a new king had been born. So they set off on a long journey with gifts, and followed the star.

On their way, the Wise Men came to King Herod's palace. "Do you know where the new king has been born?" they asked.

King Herod did not want there to be another king in the land. He was jealous. He asked the Wise Men to find Jesus, then return and tell him all about it.

The Wise Men followed the star all the way to Bethlehem, where they found Jesus with His mother Mary. They gave Jesus special gifts of gold, frankincense and myrrh. They worshiped this king who had come for all people.

God warned the Wise Men in a dream not to go back to King Herod, so they went home by a different road. And God warned Joseph to take Mary and Jesus to Egypt, where they would be safe from King Herod.

We, like the Wise Men, are led by God. We, like the Wise Men, offer God our gifts and worship. We, like the Wise Men, have been guided by God's light to Jesus, the King of all.

41

Jesus is baptized

Matthew 3:3–17; Mark 1:9–11; Luke 3:21–22; John 1:31–34

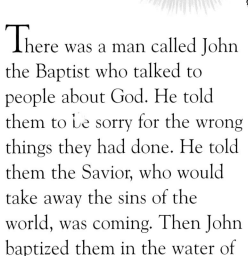

There was a man called John the Baptist who talked to people about God. He told them to be sorry for the wrong things they had done. He told them the Savior, who would take away the sins of the world, was coming. Then John baptized them in the water of the River Jordan as a sign of God washing away their sins.

When Jesus was about thirty years old, He came to see John on the bank of the river.

"I want you to baptize Me in the river," said Jesus.

John was very surprised but he baptized Jesus in the Jordan River.

As Jesus was praying, the Holy Spirit came down from heaven in the shape of a dove, and a voice from heaven spoke: "This is My Son, with whom I am pleased." It was God, the Father's, voice.

Jesus invites us to be baptized too. In Baptism Jesus, the promised Savior, washes away our sins and makes us God's own children.

42

The wedding at Cana

John 2:1–11

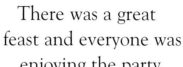

Jesus traveled around telling people about God. One day, Jesus went to a wedding at Cana in Galilee. There was a great feast and everyone was enjoying the party. Then the wine began to run out.

"You must do something," said Mary, Jesus' mother. But Jesus knew what God wanted Him to do. He told a servant to fill six large stone jars with water and take them to the man in charge of the feast. When the man tasted it, he was pleased.

"That's funny!" said the man. "People usually serve the best wine first, but you have saved the best wine for last!" Jesus' miracle was a sign that He was God's Son.

Jesus had not just turned water into wine! He showed His power and glory.

43

The soldier's servant

Matthew 8:5–13

Jesus did many miracles. These miracles were signs that Jesus was the promised Savior, the Son of God. His miracles healed people who were sick and made blind people see again. Crowds followed Him wherever He went. Jesus cared about all the people and wanted them to believe in Him as their Savior.

One day, a Roman officer begged Jesus for help. "My servant is very ill. He is too ill to leave the house."

Jesus replied, "I will go and make him well."

"No, no," said the officer. "I know that if You just say the word, he will be healed. I trust that You will heal him."

Jesus was pleased that the officer had faith in Him.

"Go home, then," said Jesus. "What you believe will be done."

The officer ran home and found to his great joy that Jesus had made his servant well again!

The terrible storm

Matthew 8:23–27

One day, Jesus and His disciples got into a boat on the lake. It had been a very busy day and Jesus was tired.

Suddenly a fierce storm came and the boat was rocked about.

The disciples were terrified, but Jesus was fast asleep in the boat.

"Save us, Lord!" they shouted to Jesus.

Jesus woke up and asked, "Why are you so afraid?"

Then Jesus told the wind and the waves to calm down.

The storm vanished.

Everyone was amazed! "Even the winds and the waves obey Him!" they said.

Jesus had saved them all from the storm on the lake.

Jesus is also with us in all our troubles. He saves us from sin, death, and the power of the devil, giving us His peace.

45

The lost sheep

Matthew 18:10–14; Luke 15:1–7

Jesus once told a parable about a shepherd and his sheep to help His disciples understand how precious His followers are to Him.

"A shepherd had a hundred sheep. He looked after them all and protected them from wild animals.

One day he found that one was missing. So the shepherd set out to find his lost sheep, leaving the 99 other sheep in the sheepfold.

He looked high and low, behind bushes and rocks. Where could the sheep be?

Suddenly the shepherd heard faint bleating; at last he had found his lost sheep!

He picked it up lovingly and carried it home on his shoulders.

He was so pleased to have found his lost sheep that he invited all his neighbors to a party."

"God is like that shepherd," said Jesus. "He cares for each one of His sheep. Each one is so precious that the Father will search for and rescue His lost children."

The lost coin

Luke 15:8–10

Jesus told another parable to help explain about His kingdom.

"A woman had ten valuable coins.

One day the woman lost one of her coins. Her house was dark. The floor was dark. But she tried to find the missing coin.

She lit a lamp, swept her house, and looked everywhere for it.

Suddenly she saw something shiny. There was the coin, lying in a dark corner.

The woman called to her friends and neighbors and said, 'Let's have a party! I am so happy to have found my lost coin!'"

"In the same way," said Jesus, "God rejoices when a sinner repents, and He helps them once again to follow Him. Each one is special, just like the woman's lost coin. God wants to keep each one as His dear children."

Jesus feeds the hungry crowd

Matthew 14:13–21; Mark 6:30–34; John 6:5–13

Jesus was once speaking to a large crowd of people. There were men, women, and children. They had been listening to Him all day and were getting hungry.

Jesus' disciples thought the people should go away and buy some food, but Jesus wanted to feed them.

"Where can we buy food for all these people?" He asked His disciples.

Philip replied, "We would need more than two hundred silver coins to buy enough!"

Andrew said, "There is a boy who says he will share his lunch. But he has only five loaves and two small fishes."

But then Jesus did a miracle. He provided what was needed. Jesus thanked God for the food then shared it among everyone! No one went away hungry. Jesus gave them all enough to eat. And there were even 12 baskets full of leftovers.

In love for us, Jesus will fill our needs too; even if we don't know how, He will do it.

49

The prodigal son

Luke 15:11–31

Jesus once told this parable to explain how much God loves us:

"There was a man who had two sons. The younger son grew bored with the countryside and had heard that the city was an exciting place. He wanted to go there. So he asked his dad for his share of his riches and set off.

His father was very sad that his son had gone away. He loved his son very much and hoped he would return.

Meanwhile, the son spent all the money very quickly, going to parties every night and having a great time. But when the money ran out, nobody wanted to be his friend any more. The son had to find a job feeding pigs. There was no food for him to eat, so he nearly ate the pig's food.

'I must go home,' he thought. 'Perhaps Dad will let me work on his farm.'

As he came near his home, he saw his dad running toward him. The father shouted: 'Welcome home!' and reached out his arms to give him a great big hug.

The father gave a great party for his son. He thought he had lost him, but the son he loved had come back. How happy that made him!"

In the same way, our heavenly Father rejoices when sinners who were lost are led to repent. He welcomes them back with open arms.

A welcome for the King

Matthew 21:1–11; Mark 11:1–10; Luke 19:29–38; John 12:12–15

Many people loved Jesus, but others were jealous of Him. They did not like the way crowds followed Him everywhere.

It was soon time for the Passover festival. Jesus spent a few days with His friends Mary, Martha, and Lazarus in Bethany.

Then, on the first day of the week, Jesus set off to the great city of Jerusalem.

Clip, clop, clip, clop, went the donkey's hooves on the road.

"Hosanna! Hurray!" shouted the crowd.

Who was this riding on a donkey? It was Jesus!

The people were so excited to see Him that they threw down cloaks in front of the donkey and waved palm branches in the air.

"Hosanna! Blessed is He that comes in the name of the Lord! Hosanna in the highest!" they shouted.

Jesus was the heavenly King who had come to save His people from sin, death, and the power of the devil. He is our triumphant King, the Savior of the world.

52

The Last Supper

Matthew 26:17–30; Mark 14:12–26; Luke 22:7–23; John 13:1–30

Jesus knew that He would not be with His friends for much longer. He wanted to celebrate the Passover meal with them one last time. Passover was a special time of remembering how God had rescued Moses and the Israelites in Egypt many years ago.

Jesus met His 12 disciples at the upper room of a house in Jerusalem.

Jesus took a bowl of water and began to wash His disciples' feet.

"You mustn't wash my feet!" said Peter. "You are our Master, not our servant!"

"Unless I wash you, you don't belong to Me," said Jesus.

They reclined at the table. The meal was lamb, bread without yeast, bitter herbs, and wine.

Jesus told them, "One of you is going to hand Me over to be killed."

"Not I!" they all said. Jesus already knew it would be Judas Iscariot.

While they were eating, Jesus took the bread, broke it, and gave it to His disciples. "Take and eat. This is My body given for you," said Jesus. "Do this to remember Me."

Then He took the cup of wine, thanked God for it, and handed it around to His disciples.

"This is My blood, shed for you for the forgiveness of sins," said Jesus. "Drink this and remember Me."

That was the first Lord's Supper. Christians continue to celebrate the Lord's Supper to receive forgiveness of sins, life, and salvation.

Jesus is arrested

Matthew 26:31–75; Mark 14:27–42; Luke 22:47–62; John 18:1–27

Jesus knew that the time was coming for Him to be taken away. He asked His disciples to come and pray with Him in the Garden of Gethsemane. But they kept falling asleep.

"Why are you sleeping?" He asked them. "Watch and pray with Me."

Suddenly a crowd came toward them, and Judas was with them. There were soldiers and chief priests. Judas came near to Jesus to kiss Him. This showed the soldiers who Jesus was. They arrested Jesus and took Him away.

Jesus' other disciples were very upset and alarmed, especially Peter. Earlier that evening, Jesus had warned Peter: "Before the cock crows tonight, you will say three times that you do not know me."

Peter had been very upset. Jesus was his friend! Peter wouldn't let Him down.

But while Peter was waiting to see what would happen to Jesus, some girls came up to him and asked if he was a friend of Jesus.

"No," said Peter, "I don't know what you are talking about!"

They asked him three times and each time he said, "No!"

Then suddenly a cock crowed. Peter remembered what Jesus had said.

Peter felt terrible that he had denied Jesus. He cried bitterly because he was so sorry for his sin.

God still loved Peter, even when he sinned.

God's love doesn't depend on what we do. Because Jesus died on the cross for us, God always loves us and forgives us. God's love doesn't change.

Jesus dies on a cross

Matthew 27:11–60; Mark 15:1–46; Luke 23:1–53; Joh 18:28–19:42

The soldiers who were guarding Jesus were very cruel to Him although Jesus had done nothing wrong. They brought Jesus before Pilate, the Roman governor. "What has this man done wrong?" Pilate asked the crowd.

"He is causing trouble all over the country," said the chief priests. "He says He is a king."

"Are You the King of the Jews?" asked Pilate.

"Yes, it is as you say," said Jesus.

"What shall I do with Jesus?" asked Pilate.

"Put Him on a cross to die!" shouted the crowd.

Pilate did not think Jesus had done anything wrong, but he wanted to please the crowd. So Pilate gave Jesus to the soldiers to be killed. The soldiers put a purple robe on Jesus and a crown of thorns on His head.

Jesus was taken by the soldiers to a place called Golgotha. There He was nailed to a cross. Above His head was a sign saying: The King of the Jews.

While Jesus was on the cross, He was still kind and loving even to those who were mean to Him.

At the ninth hour, darkness covered the land. Jesus cried out in a loud voice to God, then breathed His last breath. Jesus died. He had paid the price for our sins.

His body was taken down from the cross and placed in a tomb.

Jesus' friends thought they would never see Him again.

"Jesus is alive!"

Matthew 28; Mark 16:1–20; Luke 24; John 20; Acts 1:1–11

It had been three days since Jesus had died on the cross. All His friends were heartbroken and didn't know what to do next.

Some of the women went to His tomb early on Sunday morning, but they had a shock! The large stone blocking the entrance to the tomb had been rolled away!

They peered inside the dark tomb. Jesus' body was gone! All they could see were strips of cloth that the body had been wrapped in.

Suddenly two men in bright shining clothes appeared.

"Don't look for Jesus here," they said. "He's alive!"

The women couldn't believe it! They ran home as fast as they could and told Jesus' disciples.

Very soon they all saw Jesus again for themselves. It was true! Jesus was alive!

God had raised Jesus from the dead so we too might live forever with Him.

Over the next forty days, Jesus appeared to His friends and talked to them about the coming of God's kingdom. He ate and drank with them. "Don't leave Jerusalem," said Jesus, "but wait for the gift that God has promised to give you—the Holy Spirit. When He comes, you will be able to tell the whole world about Me!"

Then Jesus was taken up to heaven to be with God. A cloud hid Him from their eyes. Suddenly two men in white clothes stood beside Jesus' friends. "Why are you looking at the sky?" they asked. "Jesus will return one day, in the same way as you saw Him go!"

We can rejoice because we know that one day Jesus will return to take us to heaven to live with God forever.

Jesus' friends spread the Good News

Acts 1:12–2:47; 5:12–16; 9:1–19

Jesus' disciples met together to pray every day. They chose a man called Matthias to replace Judas.

On the day of Pentecost, all of Jesus' disciples met together in one place.

Suddenly there was a noise that sounded like a strong wind blowing. The noise filled the whole house. Then flames seemed to reach out and touch everyone in the room, but no one was burned. Everyone was filled with the Holy Spirit and could suddenly speak many different languages!

Although there were people in Jerusalem from every country in the world, they could all understand Jesus' disciples speaking in their own language.

Then Peter stood up and told them all about Jesus—how He had come to show God's power and do amazing things, how He had been put to death on a cross, then how God had made Him come alive again.

"Stop doing wrong and ask God to forgive you," said Peter. "Be baptized in the name of Jesus and you will be given the Holy Spirit."

That day, three thousand people were baptized.

Jesus' friends and everyone who believed in Jesus met together regularly. They prayed and ate together.

60

They shared everything they had and thanked God for their homes and food. The followers of Jesus were the first Christians.

God gave His disciples power to do miracles and heal the sick. They started to tell everyone about God. But some people didn't want to listen. There was a man called Saul who hated Christians. He wanted them all to be captured or killed. But God had a plan for Saul. One day Jesus spoke to him from heaven. Saul was blinded by a bright light. Jesus told him to go to Damascus, where a Christian called Ananias helped Saul.

Through healing and Baptism, Saul changed completely. His eyes opened and his heart was opened too. He no longer wanted to kill the Christians. In fact, he wanted to tell people about Jesus too! Saul was given a new name— Paul. He traveled far and wide, telling people about Jesus.

Jesus' followers were often in danger. But God helped them not to be afraid. They wanted people all over the world to know the amazing Good News: that God loved the world so much that He sent His Son, Jesus, to save His people.

And that amazing Good News is ours to share too.

Where to find the stories in the Bible